IMAGES OF
SPORT

QUEEN'S PARK
FOOTBALL CLUB

STADIA

IMAGES OF
SPORT

QUEEN'S PARK
FOOTBALL CLUB

BLAIR JAMES

First published 2007

STADIA is an imprint of
Tempus Publishing Limited
The Mill, Brimscombe Port,
Stroud, Gloucestershire, GL5 2QG
www.tempus-publishing.com

British Library Cataloguing in Publication Data.
A catalogue record for this book is available from the British Library.

ISBN 978 07524 4159 7

Typesetting and origination by Tempus Publishing Limited.
Printed in Great Britain.

Contents

Foreword

It is not in the least an exaggeration to claim that the history of the Queen's Park Football Club is the chronicle of the national game. For the first twenty years of their existence, that is until 1887, their word was law and they might have exercised the same dominance that the MCC did in cricket while the R and A became pre-eminent in golf.

What is perhaps more remarkable is the way in which the amateurs were able, for a century and more, to hold their own in Scottish League football, despite heavy and recurring losses to the professional ranks. In almost every case the departures have proceeded to adorn the Scottish game with other clubs, but whether they left or spent their whole career at Hampden, every player, while in a Queen's Park jersey, stood wholeheartedly for the amateur principle and upheld it worthily.

Nor did the club prove in any sense fossilised, rather it was prepared to look with interest at whatever was new. The club was far-sighted enough to construct the magnificent stadium which we know as Hampden Park, the national shrine.

The club motto, *Ludere causa ludendi*, translates happily as 'The game for the game's sake'. In this splendid book we see portrayed the great names of the past: Alan Morton, Jack Harkness and characters such as Joe Kyle and Bob Gillespie. Somewhere, unobtrusively, among these photographs may be one which will show a young man who will do great things in the game.

That will be splendid – even more so if done for 'the men with the educated feet.'

R.A. Crampsey

Acknowledgements

Many people helped me in the compilation of this book. Apologies to anyone I have unwittingly omitted.

I would like to thank the Queen's Park Football Club president and committee for giving me permission to access the Queen's Park Collection. Thanks to Richard McBrearty, curator at the Scottish Football Museum, Hampden Park, Glasgow and colleagues, particularly Kenny Strang, John Henderson, Frankie Baillie, Bob Laird, Sandy McBain, and Tommy Malcolm for their assistance and encouragement.

Peter Buchanan, Gordon Wilson, Malcolm Mackay (senior) and Jim Nicholson – all former Queen's Park players – are due credit for identifying players for me. Barry McNab provided the details of the Queen's Park Ladies players.

I would like to thank Angus Carmichael for the use of his photographs, mainly those of the 1948 British Olympic Football squad, Lady Thomson and Sandy Carmichael for access to the R.S. McColl collection, Robert Kerr for the use of the Jimmy Crawford photos, Colin Robertson for his Division Three championship 1999/2000 photograph, Mick Brady of the *Evening Times* for the Programme of the Year cover, Chris Davidson for her photographs and Keith McAllister, QPSA for the material he provided.

The Annan Gallery, *The Herald* and *Evening Times*, *The Scotsman*, *The Scottish Daily Record*,

The Scottish Daily Express, and *The Star*, Sheffield newspapers together with John Rae Photography, Forthbank News and the SNS Group have given me permission to feature photographs from their archives. Jack Murray is also due thanks for the use of his postcards.

I would particularly like to thank the photographers who have faithfully photographed the Queen's Park Football Club, season by season, home and away. Very special thanks to Dave McNeil of Queen's Park FC who spent a great deal of his valuable time monitoring all the images to ensure the highest quality possible. I am also greatly indebted to him for providing his treasure trove of negatives from the 1970s and 1980s. His images of those decades merit an exhibition of their own. He helped me greatly with the technical input to the project. Alan Rhodes, also of Queen's Park FC, has provided the images for the current era. All the photographers, known and unknown, deserve gratitude for their work, giving us an insight into this truly unique club, the Queen's Park Football Club. It has been a privilege to compile this book.

Bob Crampsey, club historian, has my thanks in providing the foreword. I am grateful for his encouragement and advice together with the information about the club which he has given to us all in his book, *The Game for the Game's Sake*. It has proved to be an invaluable reference source.

My sister, Brenda, rescued me with her secretarial skills in the layout of the text. I would like to thank my wife, Ada, for her help and patience as I spent a great deal of otherwise free time on this project. Finally, my three sons, David, Allan and Gareth, have my thanks for their support.

Every attempt has been made to trace and contact the copyright holders of all images. We will be happy to rectify any missing information in future editions.

Introduction

On a July evening in 1867, a group of young men from the north of Scotland, mainly Speyside, were out exercising in the Queen's Park Recreation ground on the south side of Glasgow. They were practising putting the shot, throwing the hammer and tossing the caber whilst all kinds of other activities were taking place around them. They noticed a group of young lads from the nearby Young Men's Christian Association kicking a ball about on the rough ground with piles of clothes being used as goalposts. The Speysiders talked to the youngsters, had their own kick about and then decided to form their own football club. Football was the game for them. The minutes of their first meeting on 9 July 1867 record this decision, the first sentence reading, 'tonight at half past eight o'clock a number of gentlemen met at No.3 Eglinton Terrace for the purpose of forming a "football club".' It was at this meeting that, following a great deal of debate, it was agreed the club should be called the 'Queen's Park Football Club'. The first rule, dated 9 August 1867, of the Queen's Park Constitution is that, 'this club shall be called the Queen's Park Football Club and its object shall be the recreation and amusement of its members.' And so began the life of the oldest football club in Scotland.

In the beginning, the club members, who paid one shilling for the privilege of entry to the club, organised games amongst themselves due to lack of opponents. On those occasions, the bachelors would take on the married men or the smokers would play the non-smokers. The club's first ever friendly game took place against Thistle FC from Glasgow Green on 1 August 1868 and Queen's Park recorded a 2-0 win. This led to an unbeaten run of almost another eight years (the ninth season of their existence) before they suffered their first defeat at the hands (and feet) of The Wanderers at The Oval in London on 5 February 1876. Prior to this event, Vale of Leven, an ambitious rival team of Queen's Park, had the honour of scoring the first ever goal against Queen's Park during a Scottish Cup tie on 8 January 1875. Vale's scorer, who entered the history books, was R. Paton.

Queen's Park Football Club has been the pioneer of football, having remained faithful to their amateur ethos which echoes the club's Latin motto *Ludere Causa Ludendi*. This translates as 'to play for the sake of playing' or, more commonly, as 'the game for the game's sake'. From 1867 to the present day the club has steadfastly remained an amateur team. At the time of writing, the club is in the Third Division of the Scottish Football League.

The importance of Queen's Park in the world game cannot be overstated. It would take many volumes to document their influence since 1867. They were innovators, regulators and missionaries. They were responsible, in part, for shaping an important part of Scotland's culture. They were The Beatles of the Victorian era with huge crowds flocking to see their adventurous style of passing football which they gave to the world. The world has not looked back as football is now a global success.

Queen's Park played in blue jerseys from the outset. They organised the first ever official international football match, Scotland versus England, in Glasgow on 30 November 1872. The Scotland team was entirely comprised of Queen's Park players. This was the first and only time that one club has provided all the players for the Scotland international team. The blue jersey of Queen's Park became the official colour of the Scotland national team. In turn, during the 1873/74 season, Queen's adopted the black and white one-inch stripe jersey. The club has used those hoop colours ever since that date. The club's nickname is The Spiders and during the earlier decades of the twentieth century the club's supporters were referred to as 'The Bowler Hat Brigade'.

Hampden Park, the home of Queen's Park and the Scotland international team, has iconic status. Due to the foresight of the Queen's Park committee members, three stadiums bearing the name of Hampden Park have been built over the last 133 years. The present ground was opened in 1903 and extended over the years until 1937, when the ground capacity was increased to 184,500 but reduced to 150,000 by the authorities. The 'Hampden Roar' was born and nowadays we can only marvel at the effect such noise must have had on opposing players. The current all-seated stadium with a capacity of 52,000 was opened, after refurbishment, in May 1999.

Queen's Park dominated the Scottish Cup competition, winning the cup on ten occasions during the first twenty years of their existence. They made consecutive appearances in the FA Cup final in 1894 and 1895, being beaten on both occasions by Blackburn Rovers. Queen's were also joint winners in 1899 of the Dewar Shield, the forerunner of the FA Charity Shield.

Queen's Park has fielded thousands of players since 1867. Many have received prominence in their day, representing Scotland at full and amateur international level. Several players have been selected for the British Olympic football team, starting with the Berlin Olympic Games in 1936. Four former Queen's Park players, namely Ian McColl, Bobby Brown, Sir Alex Ferguson and Andy Roxburgh, progressed to the position of the Scotland team manager. I have tried to feature as many players as possible in this compilation which, if you pardon the pun, can only be a snapshot of the club.

It is no exaggeration to say that the men of Queen's Park founded a sport, provided laws for it, instituted controlling bodies to govern it and kept track of its progress as it became the sport of the people. We are all greatly indebted to them.

I hope that this book will help raise the profile of the Queen's Park Football Club, the most important football club in the world.

one

The Formative Years, 1867-1900

The Queen's Park team which won the first ever Scottish Cup final. They defeated Clydesdale 2-0 on 21 March 1874. A crowd in excess of 2,000 attended. Queen's played in their usual formation of 2-2-6 with William MacKinnon scoring the first goal after a splendid piece of dribbling. His fellow forward, Robert Leckie, scored the second with a left-foot shot.

The Queen's Park team from left to right, back row: Angus MacKinnon, John Dickson, Thomas Lawrie, Charles Campbell, Robert Neill. Seated: Robert Leckie, Joseph Taylor, Harry McNeil, Joseph Thomson (captain), James Weir, William MacKinnon.

Above: Victoria Bar, 2006 – the location of the restaurant premises previously called White's at No.3 Eglinton Terrace, Glasgow. The very first meeting of Queen's Park was held at this venue on 9 July 1867.

Below: The minutes of the first meeting of 9 July 1867. The minutes begin with the evocative sentence, 'Tonight at half past eight o'clock a number of gentlemen met at No.3 Eglinton Terrace for the purpose of forming a "football club".' The rest is history…

Glasgow 9th July 1867

Tonight at half past eight o'clock a number of gentlemen met at No. 3 Eglinton Terrace for the purpose of forming a "Football Club". — After Mr. Black was called to the Chair a good deal of debating ensued and ultimately the following measures were voted for and carried, viz

First.   That the Club should be called the 'Queen's Park Football club'. —

Second.   That there should be four office bearers viz a President, Captain, Secretary and Treasurer —

Third   That there should be thirteen members of Committee including Office Bearers seven of whom to form a quorum

the following gentlemen were then duly elected as Officebearers and members of Committee viz

1	Mr Ritchie, President	9	Mr Edminston M of C
2	„ Black, Captain:	10	„ P Davidson —
3	„ Klinger, Secretary:	11	„ Gladstone —
4	„ Smith Sr Treasurer.	12	„ Reid —
5	„ Grant, Mem of Committee	13	„ Skinner —
6	„ Gardner Sr —		
7	„ Davidson R. —		
8	„ Smith Jr. —		

The Secretary then gave intimation that the Committee would meet on the 15th inst for further deliberation and to draw out a code of rules for the guidance of the Club. The Business for the evening being now finished the members retired after awarding a hearty vote of thanks to Mr. Black for his able conduct in the chair.

W. M. Klinger
Secrty.

Lewis L. Black
Chairman.

FIRST MINUTE, 1867.

10

Above: The Deaf and Dumb Institute on the edge of Queen's Park Recreation Ground. The Club stored their equipment in this building for the first six years of their existence, until they moved to the first Hampden Park in 1873. A new hospital building has been constructed on the rough playing ground at the Recreation Ground and so another piece of football history has disappeared.

Below: Acceptance of challenge game against The Thistle. In this letter of 29 July 1868, Robert Gardiner, secretary of Queen's Park, writes to accept the challenge from The Thistle (no connection to the other Glasgow club, Partick Thistle) who played at Glasgow Green. The game was to be played at Queen's Park, with twenty players on each side, and the length of the game would be no more than two hours, ends being changed after one hour if no goals were scored. And also could Thistle bring their ball in case of any breakdown? Queen's Park won 2-0 and thus began a run of seven years before they conceded a goal. The record breaker was R. Paton who scored Vale of Leven's only goal when Queen's Park defeated them 2-1 in the Scottish Cup semi-final on 8 January 1875.

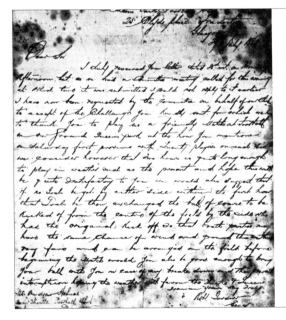

Dear Sir,

I duly received your letter dated 25th inst. on Monday Afternoon, but as we had a Committee Meeting called for this evening at which time it was submitted, I could not reply to it earlier. I have now been requested by the Committee, on behalf of our Club, to accept the challenge you kindly sent, for which we have to thank you, to play us a friendly Match at Football on our Ground, Queen's Park, at the hour you mentioned, on Saturday, first proximo, with twenty players on each side. We consider, however, that Two-hours is quite long enough to play in weather such as the present, and hope that this will be satisfactory to you. We would also suggest that if no Goals be got by either side within the first hour, that goals be then exchanged, the ball, of course, to be kicked of from the centre of the field by the side who had the origanal Kick-off, so that boath parties may have the same chance of wind and ground, this we think very fare and can be arranged on the field before beginning the Match. Would you also be good enough to bring your ball with you in case of any breake down, and thus prevent interuptsion. Hoping the weather will favour the Thistle and Queen's.

I remain,

Yours very truly,

(Sgd.) Robt. Gardner

Secy.

Queen's Park organised the first official Scotland–England international which took place at the West of Scotland cricket ground, Partick, Glasgow on 30 November 1872. The Scotland team comprised totally of Queen's Park players, the first and only occasion on which one club provided all of the players for a Scotland international team. Scotland adopted the trademark passing game of Queen's Park in their 2-2-6 formation whilst England lined up in their 1-1-8 formation. The final result, played in front of a crowd of 4,000 spectators, was 0-0. The sketches from the newspapers of the time give an impression of the incidents on and off the park. The Queen's Park players provided their own blue jerseys as the Scotland colours; they did not change to their famous black and white hoop jerseys until 1873.

The wooden pavilion of the first Hampden Park, 1873. The ground was leased from the Glasgow Corporation and the clubhouse (without running water) was erected at the cost of £21 and described at the time as a lean-to or shanty. The opening game took place on 25 October 1873 when Queen's Park defeated Dumbreck 7-0 in the first round of the Scottish Cup. This was also the first occasion on which Queen's Park played in their famous black and white hoops. Their original uniform of blue jerseys and white knickerbockers was given to the Scotland international team who, from that time forward, adopted those colours as the national colours.

    The Queen's Park line-up on that historic date was: R.W. Neil, (goal), W. Ker, J. Taylor (backs), J.J. Thomson, C. Campbell (half-backs), J.B. Weir, R. Leckie, W. McKinnon, A. McKinnon, T. Lawrie, H. McNeil (forwards). Queen's deployed their usual 2-2-6 formation.

First Hampden Park, 2006. The first Hampden Park is currently the home of the Hampden Bowling Club, Kingsley Gardens. The Cathcart Circle Railway line runs behind the clubhouse whilst a row of tenement houses, Hampden Terrace, can be seen in the background. The houses were named by the builder after John Hampden, a parliamentarian from the English Civil War! The current sign displayed at the location may have deterred the men of Mount Florida if it had been in place in 1867, then who knows what Scotland's national sport may have been.

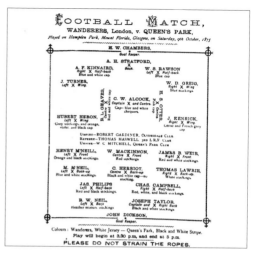

Above left: First ever Scottish Cup final medal belonging to J.J. Thomson, Queen's Park's captain in the 1873/74 Cup final.

Above right: 1875 match card of the game between Queen's Park and The Wanderers, a prominent English club of the day who, as the name suggests, did not have a home ground to call their own. The Wanderers played most home games at Battersea Park, where often the games were brought to an abrupt halt due to the park gates being closed. Queen's Park met The Wanderers in the FA Cup semi-final in London on 4 March 1872. The result was a 0-0 draw. Unfortunately, Queen's Park could not afford to return for the replay and 'scratched' from the competition. The Wanderers won the FA Cup in 1872, 1873, 1876, 1877 and 1878, when the trophy became their property. They ceased to exist in the 1880/81 season as they were unable to raise a team. Note the interesting description of each team's uniform, the common term for football outfits in Victorian times.

Above left: Charles Campbell – labelled as 'Evergreen Charlie' – was a great stalwart for Queen's Park. He was a very fine half-back and was well renowned as a prodigious header of the ball as he was able to head it as far as he could kick it. He captained Queen's Park and represented Scotland on 13 occasions. He won eight Scottish Cup medals and was a truly great pioneer for football. He accompanied James Allan of the Caledonian FC to Belfast, where on 24 October 1878 Queen's Park played Caledonian in an exhibition match at the Ulster Cricket Club. The report in *The Sportsman* on 25 October 1878 informs the reader that Queen's Park scored after only one minute's play with the Caledonian side equalising shortly before half-time. The Queen's Park team scored two more goals, making the final score 3-1 to Queen's.

There was a mixed reaction to this display of association rules, with a Dublin newspaper noting that the players were prone to head the ball 'like a pack of young goats'. However, Cliftonville FC, the first Association Club in Ireland, was born in the autumn of 1879 from this visit, and, in November 1880, the Irish Football Association was formed. After his playing days, Charles Campbell became the president of Queen's Park and from 1889 to 1890 he was president of the Scottish Football Association.

Above right: Queen's Park's 1880/81 team from left to right, back row: T. Lawrie (president), A. Watson, C. Campbell, J. Smith, J.J. Gow, T. Richmond. Middle row: H. McNeil, J.L. Kay, D. Davidson, W. Anderson. Seated: A. Rowan, A.H. Holm, M.J.E. Fraser, G. Ker.

The Queen's Park team for this season featured Andrew Watson, Scotland's first black international. He played at full-back and represented Scotland on three occasions, never being on the losing side. Scotland beat England 6-1 at The Oval, London on 12 March 1881, England's biggest home defeat by Scotland. He also won three Scottish Cup winners' medals with Queen's Park.

Opposite below, left: Match card for the game between Queen's Park and Nottinghamshire on 7 October 1876. Nottinghamshire deployed a 1-2-7 system whereas Queen's Park utilised their 2-2-6 system.

Opposite below, right: An early postcard of Queen's Park, encouraging them to play well. The Queen's Park players had to provide their own uniforms; however, by 1910 it was proving difficult to get the players to comply with this rule. The club, thereafter, provided the uniforms and washing and drying facilities.

The second Hampden Park, 1884. Due to the expansion of the Cathcart and District Railway line running through part of their first ground, Queen's Park decanted to Titwood Park, the home of Clydesdale Cricket Club, in July 1883. They played at the Titwood ground until the second Hampden, which cost £1,000 to build, was opened on 18 October 1884. On that date, Queen's Park played a friendly match against Dumbarton in front of a crowd of 7,000 spectators. According to some reports, it was a disappointing game which finished 0-0.

The report in the *Scottish Athletic Journal* of 12 January 1886 about the features of the new ground stated:

> A picture gallery has been added to the many attractions at Hampden Park. Quite a number of works in oil have been presented to the Queen's Park Club by the merchant friend of one of its most influential members and it is confidently expected that the collection will receive some valuable additions from the private galleries of the members... The exhibition will be open to the public soon.

A fine start for the new ground.

Second Hampden, 2006. When Queen's Park moved to the third (and present) Hampden in 1903, the second Hampden became the home of Third Lanark AC until their demise in February 1967. The ground was renamed New Cathkin Park but was more commonly referred to as Cathkin Park. Third Lanark and Queen's Park could not reach agreement over the sale price of the pavilion and so it was demolished! Although the terracing is overgrown, the ground is still being used in 2006 for amateur games.

Above left: 1883/84 team from left to right, back row: H. Miller, A.R. Rowan (president), R.M. Christie, W. Arnott, W. Sellar, C. Campbell, J. Smith, A.H. Holm, A. Geake, G. Gillespie. Seated: W.W. Watt, M. McDonald, J.J. Gow, W. Anderson, W. Harrower, D.S. Allan, A.P. McCallum.

Queen's were defeated 2-1 by Blackburn Rovers in the FA Cup final at The Oval, London on 29 March 1884. Queen's scorer was R.M. Christie who made his Scotland debut at the age of eighteen against England at Cathkin Park, Glasgow on 15 March 1884. Scotland won their match against England 1-0 with Christie's teammate Dr John Smith scoring the goal. Both players are featured with the Scottish Cup, which was awarded to Queen's Park due to Vale of Leven refusing to play in the final as they would be without four players on account of injuries and family bereavement. Queen's won the other trophy, the Merchants Charity Cup, when they defeated Third Lanark 8-0 on 3 May 1884.

Above right: Walter Arnott was one of Queen's Park's greatest players. A powerfully built full-back, he had an exceptional turn of speed and a very powerful shot, scoring goals from midfield. He played for Queen's Park in both their FA Cup final appearances against Blackburn Rovers at The Oval, London on 29 March 1884, when they were defeated 2-1, and again on 4 April 1885, when they were defeated 2-0. He represented Scotland on 14 occasions, including 10 consecutives games against England from 1884 to 1893.

Geordie Ker song. Geordie was a free-scoring forward who represented Scotland on five occasions, scoring in every game. This included a hat-trick on his debut for Scotland against England at the First Hampden Park on 13 March 1880, when the result was 5-4 to Scotland.

> **GEORDIE KER (The Famous Football Song)**
>
> Auld England's famed for pigeon-shooting, horsey, billiard-playing men;
> Altho' at rowin' and at cricket very few can equal them,
> When their "Roast Beef and Plum-Pudding" come upon the fitba' field,
> Tae try their skill and their endurance, tae "the Haggis" they maun yield.
> For leather-ba' manipulation whaur's the man that can compare
> Wi' the pride o' a' the Scottish nation, centre-forward – Geordie Ker!
>
> > Fancy fibbling,
> > Screwey squibbling,
> > Dodgy dribbling,
> > Always there!
> > Pass them all-ey
> > Cannon-ball-ey
> > Shot for goal-ey
> > Geordie Ker!
>
> Oor fitba' men, tho' not aesthetic, are gallant tae a high degree;
> Tae see their game most energetic, ladies are invited free.
> Some ladies doat upon the Vale, the dashing wearers o' the blue,
> While others like the speedy Rangers, colours o' a changing hue.
> But give tae me the auld Q.P. Yon's the club that I prefer,
> Wha wear the white and sable stripe, an' rear such lads as Geordie Ker.
>
> Now Englishmen pretend they ken the proper way to pass the ba'.
> They might explain the reason then they come an' coax oor lads awa'.
> If they instead o' "Beer and Beef", the "Kail and Brose" wad only try,
> They wouldna need tae come doon here oor Scottish talent for tae buy.
> Their English gold they've lang been jingling, but Queen's Park men they canna square,
> Tho' they wad gie the Bank o' England tae hae oor champion – Geordie Ker.
>
> See hoo well at Tel-el-Kebir the heroes o' the Seventy-Fourth,
> Sustained the glorious reputation of the warriors o' the North.
> There, first tae fall for Scotland's honour, died the members o' their team,
> Wha aft charged in friendly fray their rivals o' the fitba' green;
> Brave Somerville, McAllister, Dempster tae, an' mony mair,
> Has shown what brave and manly hearts are found 'mang lads like Geordie Ker.
>
> Written by Thomas Johnstone. Sung with success by J.C. Macdonald. c1884.

Queen's Park Ancients and Queen of the South Wanderers at Dumfries in 1886. 'Evergreen' Charles Campbell (front row, centre) played in what we would now call veteran football. There was just no stopping him!

1892/93 team from left to right, back row: R. McFarlane, J. Gillespie, T. Robertson, J. Hamilton. Middle row: T.S. Waddell, A. Baird, P. McCallum, E. Gillespie, and W. Gulliland. (Missing from the photograph are R. Smellie and W. Sellar.)

Queen's Park defeated Celtic 2-1 in the Scottish Cup final at Ibrox Park on 11 March 1893. This proved to be their tenth, and last, Cup final victory. It also coincided with the year in which professionalism was finally legalised in Scotland.

Thomas Waddell, outside right for Queen's Park when they won the Scottish Cup in 1893, and William Gulliland, inside right in Queen's Park's 1893 cup final-winning team. He partnered Thomas Waddell to make the left-wing partnership for Scotland against England at Goodison Park, Liverpool on 6 April 1885. Scotland lost 3-0.

A Queen's Park team of 1894/95. This was a quiet season for the team. They were defeated 4-1 by Celtic in the first round of the Scottish Cup and then beaten again 1-0 by Celtic in the semi-final of the Merchants' Charity Cup. They fared no better in the Glasgow Cup, being defeated 1-0 in round one by Rangers. Queen's Park's decision not to join the Scottish League (inaugurated on 30 April 1890) meant that they had a dearth of opponents. Queen's did not join the Scottish League until 1900.

The Queen's Park team in Copenhagen, 1898. Officials: Hugh Bennet (president), Charles Campbell, Alex Hamilton, D. Stewart. Left to right, in uniform, back row: J.F. Templeton, D. Wilson, J. Ritchie, Jock Gillespie, J. Murray. Middle row: R.A. Lambie, A.J. Christie, R.S. McColl, Dyke Berry, J.H. Irons. In front: Hugh Butler.

This photograph shows the Queen's Park party which travelled to Denmark to take part in the Intercontinental Carnival of Sports and Gymnastics, Copenhagen from 30 May to 2 June 1898.

Action shot from one of the games in Copenhagen.

Right: Tam's Pig, a memento of Queen's Park's tour of Denmark in 1898. The plaster pig is wearing Queen's colours with the dates and results of the games written on its back: Danish Boldspiel Union 0 Queen's Park 7 (30 May 1898), Danish Boldspiel Union 0 Queen's Park 3 (1 June 1898).

Below: 1898/99 team from left to right, back row: T.A. Bowie, D. Berry, David Wilson, J.F. Templeton. Middle row: C.B. Miller, (secretary), W.S. Stewart, J. Gillespie, J. Walker, J. Clarkson, A. McE. Swann. Seated: K.L. Anderson, R.A. Lambie, J. Lawrence (president), R.S. McColl, D. Stewart, J.H. Irons. Inset: W.H .Waller, A.J. Christie.

The Queen's Park team with the Glasgow Cup and the Dewar Shield (the Sheriff of London's Charity Shield). The latter trophy was the forerunner of the FA Charity Shield. Queen's played Aston Villa at Crystal Palace on 11 March 1899, with the result 0-0 after extra time. It was agreed that the trophy be shared between the two clubs. Aston Villa had possession of the trophy for the first six months and Queen's held the trophy thereafter as agreement over the next game could not be reached. It is interesting to note that the Aston Villa team was not invited to the post-match dinner.

Thomas Lawrie. President of the Scottish Football Association from 1882-1884, Lawrie joined Queen's Park in 1871 and was elected captain of the second team. He was later appointed match secretary and hon. secretary but was forced to give up the game through injury. A great orator, one said of him, 'how one small head can carry all he knows?' He was also president of the West of Scotland Amateur Athletic Association and president of the Glasgow Football Association.

Sketches of famous sporting personalities featured regularly in Victorian publications. The sketch of Thomas Lawrie is typical of these and is taken from the *Scottish Athletic Journal* of 4 April 1884.

R.S. McColl, who was nicknamed the 'Prince of Centre Forwards'. He is sporting the primrose and pink racing colours of Lord Roseberry, patron of the Scottish Football Association. The Scotland international team wore these colours in the 1900 match against England at Celtic Park, Glasgow on 7 April 1900. R.S. McColl scored a hat-trick in the 4-1 victory and was presented with the match ball.

Queen's Park players pictured with their Danish opponents in 1900. Queen's played two games on this successful tour. The results were: Danish Football Union 1 Queen's Park 6, and Danish Football Union 1 Queen's Park 8.

PRESIDENTS

MUNGO RITCHIE
1867-68

LEWIS BLACK
1868-69

JAMES C. GRANT
1869-70 1870-71

W. KEAY
1874-75 1875-76

W C MITCHELL
1876-77

ARCH RAE
1877-78

JOSEPH TAYLOR
1878-79

C. CAMPBELL
1879-80

THOMAS LAWRIE
1880-81 1881-82

RICH BROWNE
1882-83 1891-92

ARCH ROWAN
1883-84 1884 85 1890 91

A GEAKE
1885-86 1886 87 1900 01 1901 02 1902 03

A montage of Queen's Park presidents who, together with their respective committees, established the club as one of the most important football clubs in the world.

two

Onwards into the Twentieth Century, 1901 to 1920

Queen's Park *v.* Third Lanark, 1901. The 1901 International Exhibition, Kelvingrove, Glasgow opened on 2 May 1901 and ran for six months, attracting over 11 million visitors.

George McWattie, Queen's goalkeeper, was on guard in this first-round match of the Merchants' Charity Cup played on 4 May 1901 at the Exhibition Grounds, Kelvingrove. Third Lanark won 1-0.

Above: Another action shot from the Queen's Park *v.* Third Lanark match which, according to a report of the game, was played in splendid weather attracting a fairly large gate. The summer-like temperature was distinctly hard on the players.

Left: Committee badge from 1901.

Below: The Queen's Park team 1903/04. From left to right, back row: G. Miller, J.L. Logan, J.A. McLean. Middle row: J.S. Strang (secretary), J. Eadie, J.B. Taylor, J. McNaught, R.R. Hart, P.F. Jones. Seated: A. Richmond, L.H. Skene, T.F. Campbell, A. Dalzell (president), D. Wilson, E.C. Crawford, A.H. Nisbet.

Above: Ticket for the opening of Hampden Park, 1903.

Right: This postcard features David Wilson, inside left, who scored the first goal for Queen's Park in the opening game of the new Hampden Park on 31 October 1903. Queen's defeated Celtic 1-0.

DAVID WILSON, the Queen's Park forward, learned most of his football in Langside Athletic, whence he graduated to the Hampden club. He has represented the Scottish League in their English and Irish Inter-League encounters, and also played for Scotland against Wales in 1900.

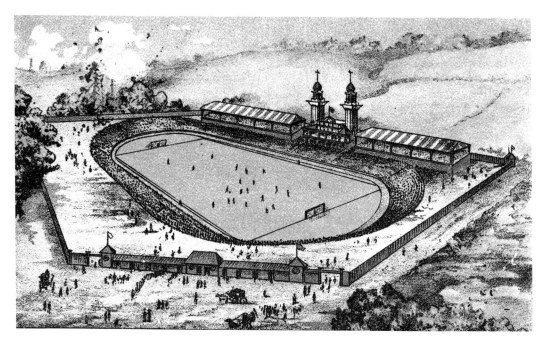

A postcard showing a view of Hampden Park shortly after its opening in 1903. The twin towers shown did not exist.

Queen's Park Ancients *v.* Scottish Rifles, 1904. This photograph shows that the Queen's Park Old Boys were still playing on!

C.V. Craigie, Queen's Park's left-back, in action at Hampden Park in the game against Rangers on 2 March 1912 which resulted in a 0-0 draw.

The Queen's Park team of 1909/10, featuring R.S. McColl (middle, back row). This was his last season with Queen's Park, making 33 appearances and scoring 18 goals. He scored six goals whilst playing at inside left against Port Glasgow Athletic in a Division One game at Hampden Park on 27 April 1910. He had previously been reinstated as an amateur in August 1907, having been a professional with Rangers until the end of the 1906/07 season.

A view of Hampden Park on 2 April 1910, when Scotland defeated England 2-0.

The
Queen's Park
Football Club,
Limited.

ADMIT TO
EAST STAND
ONLY.

S

QUEEN'S PARK *v* ENGLISH WANDERERS

THURSDAY, 1st JANUARY, 1914.

HAMPDEN PARK.   Kick-off at 1.30 p.m.

Section **F**   Seat No. 63   Row No. 4

C. B. MILLER,
JAMES STRANG,
Joint Secs.

Above: A ticket for the Queen's Park game against the English Wanderers, 1914.

Opposite above: Queen's Park team, 1911/12. From left to right, back row: M. Wilson, D.G. Drummond, J.L. McBean, F.J. Porter, T.E. Forsyth, J. Anderson, C.B. Miller (secretary). Seated: A. Couper, W. Walker, J. Clark, J. Liddell (president), J.H. McKenzie, A. Todd, E.S. Garvie. Inset: C.V. Craigie.

Eddie Garvie, pictured on the right of the front row, was a fine half-back and inside forward for Queen's. During the First World War, he enlisted with the Cameron Highlanders and died in a prisoner of war camp in Germany.

C.V. Craigie played for Queen's Park for five seasons from 1908 until 1913. He features in this photograph with teammates E.S. Garvie and J.H. McKenzie. The lone Celtic player is Patsy Gallacher.

Alan Morton pre-1920. A tricky outside left, Morton played for Queen's Park from the 1913/14 season until the 1919/20 season, when he moved to Rangers as a professional. He had a very successful career with both Rangers and Scotland. He was the scourge of the English defence as one of the Wembley Wizards, when Scotland defeated England 5-1 at Wembley on 31 March 1928. His nickname was the 'Wee Blue Devil'. His brother, Bob, played at centre forward for Queen's Park at the same time.

Queen's Park and Corinthians. The Corinthians Football Club was an amateur team based in London and formed in 1882 primarily to challenge the supremacy of Queen's Park. The Corinthians had no home ground so matches were played in and around London. A total of 70 friendly matches took place between the teams from 1886 until 1936. Queen's home games were usually played at Hampden Park on New Year's Day, attracting large crowds.

Roll of Honour 1914–1918 which lists the names of the members and players who made the supreme sacrifice during the First World War.

An early aerial view of Hampden Park.

Queen's Park 1918/19. Featured in this line-up are the Morton brothers: Bob, who played at centre forward, and Alan, an outstanding outside left.

A fine collection of gentlemen pose for the camera at the Jubilee Dinner, 1920. Held in the Grosvenor Hotel, Glasgow to mark fifty years of the Queen's Park Football Club, 1867-1917, the celebrations were delayed on account of the First World War.

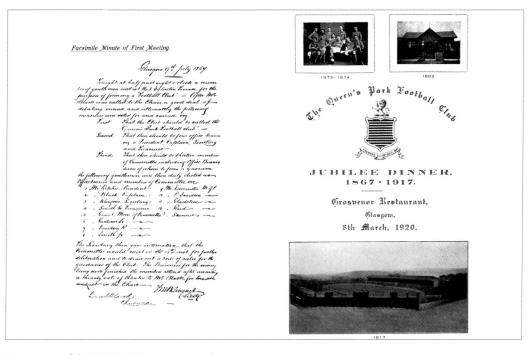

The Queen's Park Football Club

JUBILEE DINNER.
1867 · 1917.

Grosvenor Restaurant,
Glasgow,
8th March, 1920.

Front cover of the Jubilee Dinner menu card.

MENU.

Royal Whitstable Natives.

———

Mock Turtle.
Crème à la Reine.

———

Saumon Bouilli, Sauce Hollandaise.

———

Suprême de Poulet aux Riz.

———

Haggis.

———

Gigot de Mouton Rôti
Petits Pois à l'Anglaise, Pomme Chateau.

———

Faison Rôti, Salade Saison.

———

Pouding Soufflé Chocolat.
Gelée Liqueur.

———

Canapé Ecossaise.

———

Dessert.

———

Café

TOAST LIST.

THE KING,	- The President, Coun. G. T. SAMSON, *Chairman*	
Imperial Forces of Empire,	- Sir JOHN LINDSAY	
Reply,	- Col. WILSON	
The Corporation of City of Glasgow,	- Sir JOHN ANTHONY	
Reply,	Bailie JAMES CRERAR	
The Queen's Park Football Club,	- A. S. McBRIDE, Esq.	
Reply,	- CHAIRMAN	
Football Associations, League and Kindred Clubs,	- T. R. PARK, Esq.	
Reply,	THOMAS WHITE, Esq.	
The Guests,	- P. WHITE, Esq.	
Reply,	J. K. McDOWALL, Esq.	
The Press,	- Ex-Provost W. B. McMILLAN	
Reply,	{R. ROBINSON, Esq. / J. CATTON, Esq.	
Chairman,	- A. HAMILTON, Esq.	

Inside page of the Jubilee Dinner menu card.

The Queen's Park and Corinthians players assembled for a team photograph in front of the pavilion at Hampden Park in 1918. Alan Morton, with the ball in the front row, was Queen's Park's captain.

three

Mixed Fortunes, 1921 to 1940

Queen's Park 1922/23 team. From left to right, back row: J. Gossman jnr, D.S. McLay, F. Gillespie. Centre row: Arthur F. Murray (president), W.W.S. King jnr, T.S. Sneddon, J. Newton, W. Wiseman, R. Gillespie, C.J. Kelly, Hector McKenzie (secretary). Front row: J. Crawford, W. Chalmers, R. Moreland, J.B. McAlpine, H. Dickson, E.R. Scott, T.S. Pirie.

This was the team which won the Second Division title. They were undefeated at home, winning the Championship by five points.

Club sports day, 1925, which typifies the club's ethos as laid down in its constitution. The first rule dated 9 August 1867 stated, '…that this club shall be called the Queen's Park Football Club and its object shall be the recreation and amusement of its members.'

The Duke of York being introduced to the teams in front of a 60,000 crowd who attended the Queen's Park *v.* Bathgate second round Scottish Cup tie at Hampden Park on 17 January 1923. The game resulted in a 1-1 draw. Queen's Park won the replay 2-0 thanks to two goals from J.B. McAlpine.

Right: The Duke of York, the future King George VI, kicked-off the match at Hampden.

Opposite below: An action shot from the Queen's Park *v.* Corinthians game at Leyton on 12 March 1922, when the Corinthians won 2-0. R. Howard Baker, Corinthians' famous keeper, makes a save.

Queen's Park Strollers 1922/23. The Second XI has always been an important vehicle to nurture players to reach the First XI. The name The Queen's Park Strollers was adopted on 7 July 1885 on the recommendation of Mr Davis. The name has survived to the present day.

Queen's Park team 1923/24. From left to right, back row: J.B. McAlpine, W. Wiseman, R. Gillespie, T.D. Sneddon, W. Blair, W.S. King. Front row: H. Dickson, J. Crawford, W. Chalmers, R. Moreland, E.R. Scott.

Right: Jack Harkness. Harkness played in goal for Queen's Park for three seasons from 1925 until 1928, during which time he was capped on three occasions for Scotland. He appeared in the famous Wembley Wizards game against England in 1928, but whilst his teammates received a match fee of around £5, he received no payment as he was an amateur player. He moved to Heart of Midlothian as a professional in 1928 and was capped on a further nine occasions.

Below: J.B. McAlpine, whose nickname was 'Mutt' after a newspaper cartoon character of the day, had a long and distinguished career with Queen's Park from 1919 until 1933. He held the record of the most appearances until Ross Caven came along in the 1980s.

Left: Newspaper report of Laurie McBain's exceptional feat of scoring six goals for Queen's Park against Partick Thistle at Firhill on 8 February 1927. This equalled R.S McColl's club record when he scored six goals against Port Glasgow Athletic on 26 April 1910.

Below: Club crest. The coat of arms granted to the Queen's Park Football Club displays the club's Latin motto, *Ludere Causa Ludendi*, which means to play for the sake of playing or, as it is more commonly referred to, 'the Game for the Game's sake'.

Opposite above: Lesser Hampden. Formerly part of the Clincart Farm dating from the nineteenth century, Queen's Park opened this ground, which is adjacent to the main stadium, in 1925. The ground is used by the minor teams connected to the club such as The Strollers. The original farmhouse building is still in place and is now being used for the team changing rooms. It makes quite an interesting contrast to the facilities available at the main stadium.

Opposite below: J.B. McAlpine introducing the Queen's Park players to King Christian of Denmark prior to a game against the Danish national team in 1925. The Queen's Park players in this line-up include K. Campbell, W. Wiseman, R. Gillespie, D. McLelland, W.S. King, J. Crawford and E.R. Scott. Queen's Park won 5-0.

Jimmy Crawford played for Queen's Park from 1923 to 1936. He gained five full Scotland caps and represented the Scottish League on three occasions.

Jimmy Crawford, Queen's Park's flying winger, was indeed a champion sprinter. He equalled the 100-yard sprint record of ten seconds flat at the Scottish Amateur Athletics Championship on 2 June 1929.

Jimmy Crawford sprinting over the line at the sprint event held at Hampden Park.

Above: Jimmy Crawford leading the Queen's Park team out of the tunnel at Hampden Park. J.B. McAlpine and T.G Smith follow the leader.

Below: 1929/30 team from left to right, back row: P. Doig (secretary), Hugh Logan, J.M. Fullarton, W.O. Walker, W.S. King, T.G. Smith, W. Wiseman, J.M. Dodds, L. Fitzgerald, F.J. McConaghy, R.G.C. Peden, R. Manderson (trainer). Front row: J. Crawford, F.P. Taylor, T.K. Campbell, J.B. McAlpine, J.P.W. Steel (president), R. Gillespie, C.D. MacKenzie, R. Grant, J. MacDonald.

In view of the intense interest in Saturday's big Cup-tie between

QUEEN'S PARK
and
RANGERS

we would suggest that News-agents should send their orders for extra supplies immediately.

MONEY IN THE CUP

	Attendance.	Receipts.
*Queen's Park v. Rangers	95,722	£4000
Dundee v. Morton	15,000	530
Hearts v. Clydebank	15,000	617
Raith Rovers v. Aberdeen	10,000	500
St Bernard v. Third Lanark	10,000	350
†Caledonian v. Celtic	6,500	248
Ayr v. Mid-Annandale	5,500	210
Buckie Thistle v. Falkirk	4,300	240
East Fife v. Queen of the South	4,500	180
Dumbarton v. Cowdenbeath	4,500	170
Motherwell v. East Stirlingshire	4,000	145
Albion Rovers v. Alloa	3,600	140
Clyde v. Keith	2,000	138
Forfar Athletic v. Brechin City	3,000	130
Hibernian v. Leith Amateurs	3,300	128
Kilmarnock v. Paisley Acas.	3,000	125
Airdrieonians v. Dunfermline	3,226	122
Falkirk Amateurs v. Leith Athletic	3,000	120
King's Park v. Bathgate	3,000	110
Stranraer v. Dundee United	2,500	100
Bo'ness v. St Johnstone	2,500	98
Hamilton v. Stenhousemuir	2,000	95
Dalbeattie Star v. Partick Thistle	2,100	86
St Cuthbert's Wan. v. St Mirren	1,500	67
Arbroath v. Galston	1,700	60
Montrose v. Solway Star	1,300	60
Peterhead v. Vale of Leithen	1,400	48
Nithsdale W. v. St Andrews Univ.	800	30
Murrayfield Amat. v. Burntisland Shipyard	500	18
Royal Albert v. Beith	600	12
Civil Service S. v. Clachnacuddin	150	4½

* First Round Record for Britain.
† Inverness Record.

Above: Queen's Park's first round Scottish Cup tie against Rangers at Hampden Park on 18 January 1930 was greatly anticipated by the fans. This newspaper advert in the run-up to the game recommends the placing of orders for extra copies.

Left: Gate receipts for the other games in the first round of the Scottish Cup on 18 January 1930. Makes interesting reading.

Opposte below: Scotland Amateur International team, 1933. Queen's Park provided the majority of players for the Scottish Amateur International team. The fixture against Ireland at Celtic Park on 28 January 1933 proved to be no exception as Queen's Park provided seven of the team in this line-up. From left to right, back row: A. Anderson (Queen's Park), A. Kerr (Third Lanark), Lieut Harvey (The Army), T.G. Smith (Queen's Park), W. Hamilton (Edinburgh City), J. Parlane (Dumbarton), J. Qusklay (trainer, Celtic). Front row: J. Crawford (Queen's Park), J.M. Dodds (Queen's Park), A. McCartney, (Queen's Park), J. Gardiner (Queen's Park), T.K. Campbell (Queen's Park). Scotland won 6-0.

Right: R.S. McColl, a Queen's Park legend, delivers his verdict on the game which attracted a record crowd of 95,772. This is a record for an amateur team playing senior football and still stands as Queen's record home attendance.

Rangers defeated Queen's Park 1-0 in what proved to be a disappointing game.

Above: The Scotland team which played in front of a record crowd of 136,259 against England at Hampden on 1 April 1933. The attendance was a world record at that time. Bob Gillespie, Queen's Park, was drafted in at the last minute which meant two amateur players, Crawford and Gillespie, were represented in the full international team. From left to right, back row: Wilson (Celtic), McPhail (Rangers), Anderson (Hearts), Jackson (Partick Thistle), McDonald (Celtic), Brown (Rangers). Front row: Crawford (Queen's Park), McGrory (Celtic), Gillespie (Queen's Park), Marshall (Rangers), Duncan (Derby County).

Scotland won 2-1 with Jimmy McGrory scoring both of their goals.

Left: Bob Gillespie was centre half and captain of Queen's Park and played for the club from 1918 to 1933. In his last season for Queen's Park he was drafted in at late notice to captain the full Scotland team against England at Hampden on 1 April 1933. He replaced the injured Davie Meiklejohn of Rangers. Bob was the last amateur player to captain Scotland.

Opposite below: Hibernian *v.* Queen's Park, 11 January 1936. An incident during the match at Easter Road, Edinburgh between Hibernian and Queen's Park, when Queen's Park won 1-0 thanks to the goal from Joe Kyle. The Queen's Park goalkeeper, Desmond White, can be seen snatching the ball from the feet of an opposing forward during a Hibernian attack. Desmond White, in later years, was appointed secretary of Celtic FC.

Above: An Edinburgh City and Queen's Park select played against a combined Hearts and Hibernian team to mark the opening of Edinburgh City's ground at East Pilton in August 1935.

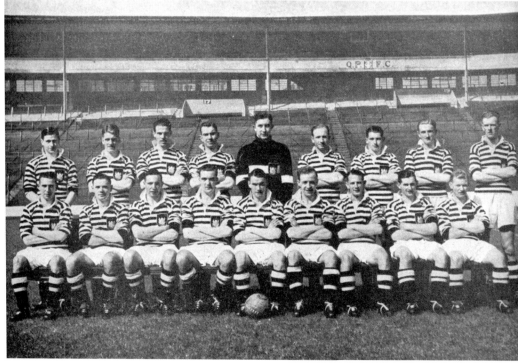

Above left: George Wylie, stylish doorman who welcomed all to Hampden Park in the 1930s.

Above right: Jimmy Ritchie, the hardworking groundsman who was exemplary in looking after the playing surface at Hampden Park. He successfully managed to fend off a ploughing order for Lesser Hampden during the Second World War.

Opposite above: Olympic Games, Berlin, 1936. Four Queen's Park players were chosen for the Great Britain football team in the Olympic Games at Berlin in August 1936. From left to right, back row: J. Crawford, J.M. Dodds, J. Gardiner, J.R. Kyle. Front row: W.S. King (QPFC travelling representative), P. Doig (QPFC president), B. Manderson (British team masseur).

Opposite below: 1937/38 Queen's Park team. From left to right, back row: R.G.D. Gordon, D.J.R. Cheyne, W.D. Buchanan, W.S. MacDonald, D. White, T. Young, A. Rae, J.M. Brown, W. Browning. Front row: S.S. Duncan, J.R. Kyle, R.M. Cross, W. Martin, A. Hosie (captain), J. Gardiner, T.K. Campbell, W.J.D. Kinghorn, D. Christie.

In the first full season at the Greater Hampden Park, completed at the cost of £156,000, Queen's finished in twelfth position out of twenty in the Scottish League Division One. Willie Martin notched up his thirtieth goal during the last game of the season in the 1-1 draw with Hamilton Academical.

Above left: J.M. (Mac) Dodds, a stalwart centre forward who played for Queen's from 1928 until 1937, making 221 appearances and scoring 141 goals. He played in the British Olympic football team at the Berlin Olympics in 1936.

Above right: Joe Kyle, an inside forward who played for Queen's Park for ten seasons from 1933 until the end of season 1942/43. He scored 14 goals for Queen's in seasons 1936/37, 18 in 1938/39 and 22 in 1939/40. He also played for the Great Britain football team in the Berlin Olympics of 1936.

Above right: Willie Martin was a free-scoring inside forward who played for Queen's Park from 1933 until 1938. After scoring 30 goals for Queen's in the 1937/38 season, he moved to Clyde, where he won a Scottish Cup winners' medal when Clyde beat Motherwell 4-0 in the 1939 cup final. He scored two of the goals.

Above left: Dr Alec Cross. A highly-rated left half who played from 1938 until the end of season 1946/47, when injury curtailed his career.

Left: Mustapha Mansour, Queen's Park's Egyptian goalkeeper who made 49 appearances for The Spiders between 1937 and 1939. He had been studying at Jordanhill College in Glasgow when he joined Queen's.

Below: Queen's Park *v.* Airdrie, 1939. The Airdrie goalkeeper keeps his bonnet on as he clutches the ball following a Queen's Park attack.

four

Down, Up and Down, 1941 to 1960

1955/56 Queen's Park team from left to right, back row: D.H. McLean, W.L. Ross, I.G. Harnett, R.L. Cromar, J.C. Valentine, W. Gibson (trainer). Middle row: J.M. Reid, G. Church, D. McD. Orr, W.L. Black, F.C. Crampsey, J.F. Robb, A. Glen, G. Savage, N.C. Hopper. Seated: A.P. McEwan, C. Church, R.G. McCann, W.M. Hastie (captain), R. Dalziel, W. Omand, J.H. Devine.

This team won the Scottish League 'B' Division Championship scoring 78 goals for a loss of 28 goals over the season. Top scorer was centre forward Charlie Church, who scored 17 goals. He was closely followed by Hunter Devine, scoring 14.

Above: Aerial photograph of Hampden Park.

Left: This advert highlights that the London Midland Scottish railway company provided a regular service of 'Football Specials' between Glasgow Central and Mount Florida stations.

Bobby Brown made his debut for Queen's Park in a Southern League game against Celtic on 13 April 1940 which resulted in a 4-4 draw. He remained with the club until the end of the 1945/46 season, when he moved to Rangers as a successor to Jerry Dawson. During the Second World War he played as a guest for Portsmouth, Chester and Chelsea. With Queen's Park he gained a full international cap against Belgium on 23 January 1946 and a further five caps when he was playing for Rangers. He was the Scotland team manager from February 1967 until July 1971.

Tony Harris. A forward with Queen's Park for five seasons from 1940/41 to 1945/46, Harris moved to Aberdeen, where he won a Scottish Cup winners' medal in the 2-1 victory over Hibernian in the 1947 final.

Johnny Aitkenhead. He played at outside left, scoring over 100 goals in his spell at the club from 1941/42 until the end of the 1945/46 season when he moved to Hibernian. He later transferred to Motherwell.

Colin Liddell played primarily at centre forward for Queen's Park from 1942/43 until the end of season 1946/47 when he moved to Greenock Morton. He featured in the Morton team which was defeated 1-0 in the 1948 Scottish Cup final by Rangers after a replay. Both games were played at Hampden Park, attracting a crowd of 129,176 for the first game and 131,975 for the replayed game the following Wednesday.

Hampden's Cup-Spinning Spiders

I. M'COLL.   R. CALDWELL,   A. CROSS.   L. HODGE.   A. MACAULAY.

J. STEADWARD.   J. M'COLL.   W. GALBRAITH.   J. HARRIS.   A. DIXON.   J. AITKENHEAD.

Above: Newspaper strip of photographs from 1945 of the Queen's Park players, including Ian McColl who played at right half for two seasons for Queen's Park. He made his debut on 23 October 1943 against Hearts, who won 9-0 – the least said about that the better! He moved to Rangers where he gained 14 caps for Scotland. In November 1960 he was appointed the Scotland team manager whilst still a player. In May 1965 he was succeeded by Jock Stein, Celtic's manager.

Right: Ronnie Simpson made his debut, aged fourteen years and 304 days, in goal for Queen's Park in the Summer Cup tie against Clyde on 2 June 1945. Queen's won 5-2. Ronnie played for Queen's until the end of the 1949/50 season when he moved to Third Lanark. At the end of the following season he moved to Newcastle United where he won two FA Cup winners' medals in 1952 and 1955. He returned to Scotland to play for Hibernian, later moving to Celtic. He had an extraordinary career, gaining a European Cup winners' medal in 1967 when playing with Celtic. To cap it all, he made his debut for Scotland, at the age of thirty-six, against England at Wembley in 1967 when Scotland beat the World Cup holders 3-2.

1947/48 Queen's Park XI. This was the line-up on the opening day of the season, 13 August 1947, when Queen's suffered a home defeat of 5-2 by Motherwell. From left to right, back row: D. Letham, A. Miller, J.S. Hardie, R.C. Simpson, D. McBain, A. Carmichael. Front row: T. Alexander, H.G. Miller, J. Farquhar, R.H. Gunn, J.M. Brown.

British Olympic football team, London, 1948. From left to right, standing: D. Letham, J. Rawlings, E.R. Neale, J. Smith, A.M. Carmichael, H.J. McIlvenny, A.I. Aitken, J. McColl. Seated: R.W. Phipps, G.T. Manning, A.H. Hopper, T. Curry (trainer), M. Busby (manager), J.R.E. Hardisty (captain), E.G. Lee, D.M. McBain. Front row: D. Kellecher, W.G. Amor, F.J. Donovan, E.G. Fright, F.P. Kippax, J.A. Boyd, R.C. Simpson.

Seven Queen's Park players were part of the Great Britain football squad. They were Davie Letham, Angus Carmichael, Andy Aitken, Jimmy McColl, Dougie McBain, Alan Boyd and Ronnie Simpson. The team was managed by Matt Busby of Manchester United. The Great Britain team were beaten 3-1 by Yugoslavia in the semi-finals. In the play-offs for the bronze medal, Great Britain were defeated 5-3 by Denmark. Ronnie Simpson, Angus Carmichael, Alan Boyd and Andy Aitken took part in that game.

Right: Newspaper report of the game between Walthamstow Avenue and Queen's Park, Easter 1951. The Queen's Park team was the first Scottish team to appear in a live television broadcast in a game against Walthamstow Avenue which attracted an audience of 200,000 viewers. Queen's Park won 2-0 with Derek Grierson scoring both goals.

Below: Queen's Park *v.* Celtic in the Glasgow Cup replay at Hampden Park on 3 September 1952, with a crowd of 20,000 in attendance. Celtic's Willie Fernie tackles Queen's goalkeeper, Hastie Weir. The final score was 2-2, with Queen's winning the tie by the toss of a coin.

Hampden couldn't hold 'crowd' that saw Q.P. win

By Martin Lee

WALTHAMSTOW AVENUE .. 0 QUEEN'S PARK 2

QUEEN'S PARK played before what was probably the biggest football "audience" in Britain yesterday—thanks to the bad weather!

Explanation was that on this, their first post-war visit to London, the Hampden team's game with the Isthmian League club Walthamstow Avenue, was televised and it is estimated that over 200,000 viewers saw the game.

This match was the highlight in Walthamstow's jubilee celebrations this season, but Queen's Park weren't having any of that!

Walthamstow were a poor team compared with the Division "B" side and I felt that Queen's Park would have won far more easily had there been something vital at stake. With inside-forward trio Dalziel, Grierson, and O'Connell in sparkling form the Walthamstow half-back line found themselves moving backwards most of the time.

The two goals both came from international GRIERSON, the first after 25 minutes when Dalziel sold a perfect dummy in allowing a pass from Brown to run on to Grierson and the little centre forward cracked the ball home from 18 yards.

Defence erred

The second came 5 minutes before half-time after a mistake by the Walthamstow goalkeeper and centre-half. Each left it to the other to clear but Grierson raced in and stuck out a foot to toll the ball slowly into the net.

The London club fought back in the second-half with amateur international Jim Lewis—chosen to lead England at Hampden Park on April 7—the star forward.

Queen's Park—S. H. Weir, H. Little C. Imlah, A. Bell, O. S. Harbour, W. M. Hastie, R. McKinlay, S. O'Connell, D. D. Grierson, R. Dalziel, R. M. Brown.

Above: Queen's Park *v.* Rangers in the Glasgow Cup semi-final on 9 September 1952, which Queen's lost 2-0. Derek Grierson had transferred to Rangers at the beginning of the season and here he was playing against some of his former teammates.

Left: The ball from the opening game of the New Hampden Park on 31 October 1903. Queen's Park goalkeeper Dr Leslie Skene held on to the ball after the final whistle in the game with Celtic. He kept the ball at his home in Douglas, Isle of Man until 1933 when he returned it to its home at Hampden Park. The ball is pictured receiving a makeover for the fiftieth anniversary celebrations and has been displayed at the Scottish Football Museum, Hampden Park.

Queen's Park *v.* Motherwell, 8 February 1956. Fifth round of the Scottish Cup at Firs Park, Motherwell. Alec Glen in only his sixth first-team appearance scores a penalty, beating ex-Queen's Park goalie, Hastie Weir. Junior Omand scored another goal in the eighty-eighth minute to give Queen's a 2-0 victory.

Hibernian *v.* Queen's Park. Willie Hastie (Queen's Park) with Gordon Smith (Hibs) in this game at Easter Road, Edinburgh on 6 October 1956 which ended in a 1-1 draw with Bert Cromar scoring the equalising goal. The Hibs forward line included Gordon Smith, Eddie Turnbull and Lawrie Reilly.

Third Lanark *v.* Queen's Park in the third round of the Scottish Cup, played at Cathkin Park on 1 March 1958. Third Lanark won 5-3.

Junior Omand, playing at inside left for Queen's Park, is thwarted by Third Lanark's diminutive goalkeeper, Jocky Robertson, famed for his acrobatic saves. Geoff Slingsby of Third Lanark looks on. Junior Omand played primarily as an outside left and latterly as an inside forward during his eleven seasons with Queen's Park from the 1951/52 to 1962/63 season.

Opposite above: Sheffield FC Centenary, 1957. Willie Hastie (Queen's Park) introducing Prince Philip to Frank Crampsey and Ian Harnett prior to the Centenary match between Sheffield FC and Queen's Park at Bramall Lane, Sheffield in October 1957. T. Kerr Campbell, president of Queen's Park, is following Prince Philip.

Opposite below: Action shot from the Centenary match for Sheffield FC. Frank Crampsey tips a shot over the bar. The score was 2-2 with Hunter Devine and Malcolm Darroch scoring the goals for Queen's Park. Sheffield FC, nicknamed 'The Club', was formed on 24 October 1857, and has been recognised by the Football Association as the oldest club in the world. The Club bears no relation to either Sheffield United or Sheffield Wednesday.

Queen's Park *v.* Aberdeen. Paddy Buckley (Aberdeen) and John Valentine (Queen's Park) watch the ball go past. Queen's were defeated 2-0 in this game at Hampden which attracted a crowd of 12,185.

Queen's Park, season 1958/59. From left to right, seated: J. Gilroy, W. Omand, I.G. Harnett, (captain), T. Kerr Campbell (president), D.H. McLean, I. Clark, A.C. Ferguson. Middle row: F. Lyon (assistant trainer), K.C. McAlpine, R.L. Cromar, G. Falconer, R. McKinven, W.J. Pinkerton, R.K. Johnstone, P. Kane, C. Church, W. Gibson (trainer), A. Turpie, W. McBride, W. Bell, W. Williamson (coach). Back row: I.K. Drainer, M. Darroch, R.M. Wood.

This line-up includes Alex Ferguson, who began his senior career at Queen's Park, making his First XI debut at Stranraer on 15 November 1958, scoring Queen's only goal in a 2-1 defeat. He moved to St Johnstone as a professional in 1960. He later moved to Dunfermline, Rangers, Falkirk and Ayr. He began his managerial career at East Stirling, then St Mirren, Aberdeen and Manchester United. He was manager of the Scotland team which qualified for the World Cup finals in Mexico in 1986.

five

Division Two Regulars, the 1960s

Partick Thistle *v.* Queen's Park. Peter Buchanan, Queen's centre forward, in action against Partick Thistle in the first round of the Glasgow Cup at Firhill on 22 August 1960. Thistle's goalkeeper, Steadward, George Boardman and Jim Hewlett, both of Queen's Park, watch the ball go past. Peter Buchanan scored Queen's only goal in the 5-1 defeat.

The front cover of a programme for the inaugural game on 17 October 1961 when Rangers played Eintracht Frankfurt in a friendly match to mark the installation of the floodlights at Hampden Park. Eintracht Frankfurt won 3-2 in front of a crowd of 104,679 which was the first six-figure attendance for a friendly game. It cost £30,000 to install the floodlights. It is interesting to note that in 1961 the electricity bill for a game entirely under floodlights was £15.

Queen's Park players testing floodlights at Hampden Park in October 1961. The first full game played under the new floodlights by Queen's Park was a mid-week game on Wednesday 22 November 1961, when Queen's drew 1-1 with Hamilton Academical. Douglas Logan was Queen's scorer. Queen's Park played their first game 'under electric light' at the first Hampden on 6 November 1878 in a friendly game against Vale of Leven. Reports tell of one light with the strength of 6,000 candles and another two, each of 1,200 candle strength, illuminating the ground. The south-west corner of the ground, unsurprisingly, was reported as being 'gloomy'.

1961/62 Queen's Park team. From left to right, standing: J. Gillies (secretary), D.A. Grant, R.L. Cromar, C. McG. Gilmour, D.C. Logan, W.J. Pinkerton, I.M. Donaldson, W. Neil, J.S. Cole, W. Omand, W. Gibson (trainer), F. Lyon (assistant trainer). Front row: W. Telfer, G. Boardman, P.G. Buchanan, J. Gardiner (president), N.C. Hopper, D.A. Houston, A. Roxburgh.

This team line-up includes Andy Roxburgh who played as a forward for Queen's Park for two seasons from 1961/62 to 1962/63. He moved on to play for Partick Thistle, Clydebank and Falkirk before joining the SFA coaching staff, where he eventually became head of coaching. He was appointed as the Scotland team manager in 1986 and remained in that post until 1993. He moved to UEFA as technical director in 1994.

MALKY MACKAY

Malcolm Mackay, who was affectionately known as Malky Mackay. On his debut for Queen's Park First XI on 29 August 1962 against Queen of the South, he scored all four goals in the 4-4 draw. Follow that! He did. He scored a hat-trick in his next game against East Fife at Methil on 1 September 1962 when Queen's lost 5-4. A goal-scoring forward, he scored 163 goals in 402 appearances from season 1962/63 to season 1975/76. A great servant for the club on and off the park.

THE FOOTBALL ASSOCIATION CENTENARY YEAR

~1863~

~1963~

AMATEUR INTERNATIONAL TOURNAMENT

13TH · 22ND MAY 1963

TOURNAMENT   PROGRAMME   PRICE   ONE   SHILLING

Programme for the Centenary of the FA 1963 Amateur International Tournament which took place in England. The Scotland team, which comprised mainly Queen's Park players, won Group A, which also included Italy, the Republic of Ireland and Switzerland. The teams in Group B, which was won by West Germany, also included England, France and the Netherlands. Scotland defeated West Germany 5-2 in the final, thus qualifying to take part in the football tournament as part of the Kenyan independence celebrations in December 1963.

'Hampden Roar' cartoon. The 'Hampden Roar' was born in the 1930s. The shouts of encouragement from a 140,000-plus crowd created a huge wall of sound which must have been a terrifying noise for many of Scotland's opposing players to deal with, and was often reckoned to be Scotland's 'twelfth man'.

Another cartoon from the Supporters' Association notebook.

KENYA
INDEPENDENCE CELEBRATIONS

Amateur
International
Tournament

7th - 15th DECEMBER, 1963

TRAVEL ARRANGEMENTS
For Scottish Team and Officials, etc.

Amateur Scotland players and officials travelled to Kenya for the Kenya Independence Celebrations Tournament, 7-15 December 1963. Scotland defeated Uganda 3-0 and Tanganyika 7-2 to reach the final against Kenya. Kenya won 3-2. Scotland's top scorer was seventeen-year-old Peter Lorimer of Leeds United with six goals.

Queen's Park 1964/65, from left to right, back row: M.D. Mackay, L. Gibson. Middle row: J. Gillies (secretary), C. Gilmour, J. Pollatschek, R.B. Clark, W. Carter, J. McLaughlin, J. Stewart, I. Robertson, J. Brown. Seated: N.C. Hopper, D. Miller, P.G. Buchanan, D. Letham (president), W. Neil (captain), A. Ingram, M. Hay.

Hamilton Academical *v.* Queen's Park. Winter conditions prevailed in this game on Boxing Day 1964 at Douglas Park, Hamilton. The game resulted in a 2-0 victory for Queen's with goals from Paul Breslin and Malky Mackay.

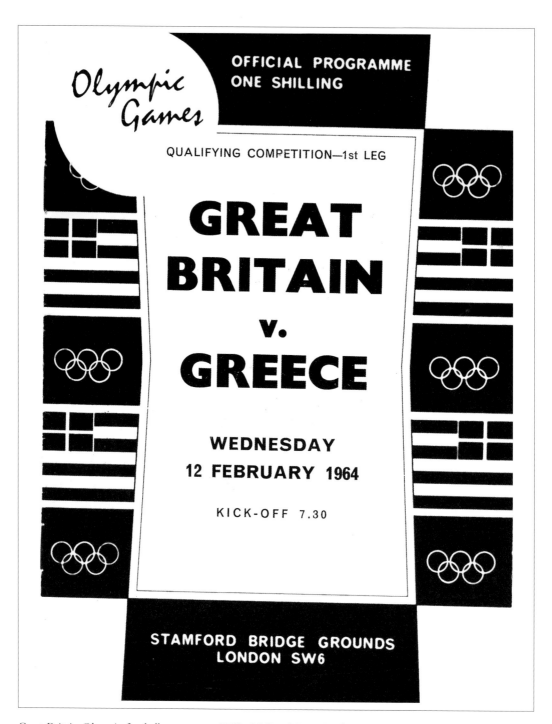

OFFICIAL PROGRAMME
ONE SHILLING

Olympic Games

QUALIFYING COMPETITION—1st LEG

GREAT BRITAIN

v.

GREECE

WEDNESDAY
12 FEBRUARY 1964

KICK-OFF 7.30

STAMFORD BRIDGE GROUNDS
LONDON SW6

Great Britain Olympic football programme. Willie Neil and Peter Buchanan were selected for the qualifying ties with both featuring in the first-round win against Iceland. Peter Buchanan played in the second-round game against Greece at Stamford Bridge, scoring Great Britain's second and winning goal in the 2-1 victory. However, Greece won the return 4-1 and so ended Great Britain's hopes of taking part in the Olympic Games in Tokyo.

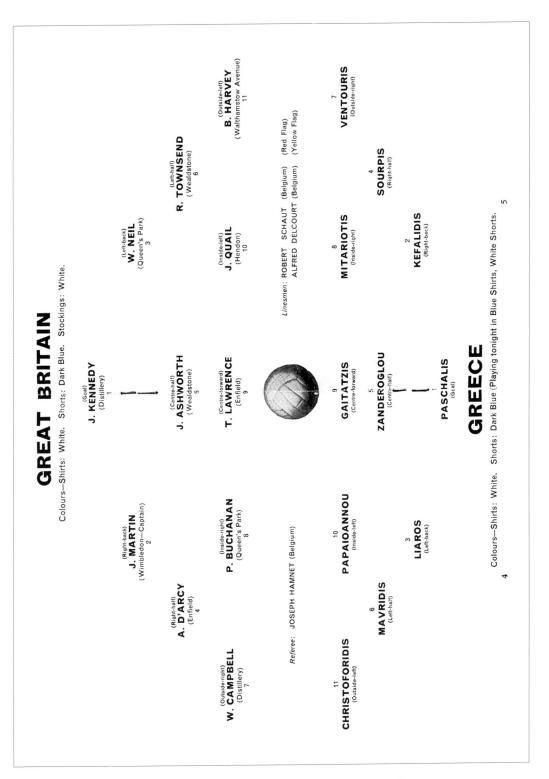

The inside of the programme showing the team line-ups for Great Britain against Greece.

Mokwa Football Athletic Club, Northern Nigeria. T.C. Moffat, Ministry of Agriculture, Suva, Fiji, wrote to Queen's Park to request a set of jerseys for the Mokwa Football Athletic Club, Niger Province, Northern Nigeria. The strips were duly provided to Mr Lashiola. Queen's Park continues to foster football around the world.

Gordon Wilson, Queen's Park goalkeeper, makes a vital save in the Scottish Cup replay tie on 20 February 1967 at Broomfield against Airdrie, which earned Queen's a quarter-final tie against Celtic at Celtic Park on 11 March 1967. In that game, Queen's went ahead in the first minute, thanks to an own goal by Tommy Gemmell of Celtic and, although Niall Hopper scored for Queen's in thirty-one minutes, Queen's were 4-2 down at half-time. Almost from the kick-off, Niall Hopper made the score 4-3. A late winner from Celtic made the score 5-3. Celtic went on to greater things later in the season when they became the first British club to win the European Cup.

1966/67 Queen's Park First XI. From left to right, standing: J. Gillies (ground secretary), H. Davis (trainer), P.G. Buchanan, E. Hunter, J. Roddie, D.S. Holmes, J. Taylor, G. Wilson, I. Campbell, I. Robertson, P. Conn, J.L. Pollatschek, J. McLaughlin, R. Baxter (assistant trainer). Seated: C. Emery, T. Barr, N.C. Hopper, M.A. Hay, B. Russell, (president), W. Neil (captain), M. Mackay, W. Carter, C. Gilmour.

The team had a successful run in the Scottish Cup, being defeated by Celtic 5–3 in an exciting round three game.

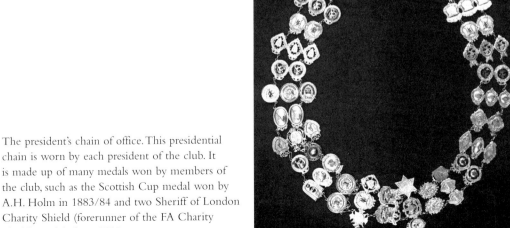

The president's chain of office. This presidential chain is worn by each president of the club. It is made up of many medals won by members of the club, such as the Scottish Cup medal won by A.H. Holm in 1883/84 and two Sheriff of London Charity Shield (forerunner of the FA Charity Shield) medals from 1899.

QUEEN'S PARK F.C. CENTENARY
1867 – 1967

QUEEN'S PARK

Versus

BRITISH AMATEUR SELECT

Hampden Park, Friday, 4th August, 1967. Kick-off 7.30 p.m.

GRAND CHALLENGE MATCH

CELTIC

Versus

TOTTENHAM HOTSPUR

Hampden Park, Saturday, 5th August, 1967. Kick-off 3 p.m.

SOUVENIR PROGRAMME 1/-

Cover of the programme for the Queen's Park Centenary games on 4 and 5 August 1967.

The Queen's Park Football Club Ltd.

(FOUNDED 9th JULY 1867)

CENTENARY BANQUET

CITY CHAMBERS

GLASGOW

SATURDAY, 5th AUGUST, 1967

Menu cover for the Queen's Park Centenary dinner at the City Chambers, Glasgow.

Left: Window display at 312 Duke Street, Glasgow, highlighting the Centenary of Queen's Park.

Below: The Scotland amateur team leaving for the European Amateur Competition in Majorca, June 1967. Queen's Park provided most of the players. Scotland lost to Austria in the final game in Palma. From the top: John Taylor, Jimmy Graham (Glasgow University), Iain Campbell, Brian Mulgrew, Tommy Barr, George Cumming (Partick Thistle), Wilson Carter, Millar Hay, Charlie Gilmour, Niall Hopper, Eddie Hunter, Ian Robertson, Malky Mackay, Gordon Wilson, John McLaughlin, Harold Davis (coach), Willie Neil (all Queen's Park except where stated).

six

More of the Same, the 1970s

Queen's Park season 1971/72, from left to right, standing: J. Gillies (secretary), A. McEwan (physiotherapist), F. Thomson, T. Barr, P. Dawson, J.M. Hastie, J. Taylor, I. Robertson, A. MacDonald, R. Malloy, C. Smith, W. Currie, T. Duncan (coach). Seated: G. Colgan, I. Campbell, R. Morrison, E. Hunter (captain), J. Brown (president), J. Borland, W. Whyte, A. Stamp, M.D. Mackay.

Left: Bobby Cameron was Queen's Park's goalkeeper for five seasons from 1973/74 to 1977/78 making 131 appearances.

Below: An aerial view of Hampden Park in 1972; the three Hampden Parks can be seen. The first Hampden Park is located on the edge of the Queen's Park Recreation Ground (top left of picture), and then the second Hampden is found at the top of the photograph just above the site of the third Hampden Park.

Queen's Park 1973/74. From left to right, standing: J. Gillies (ground secretary), G. Colgan, E. Hunter, M. Mackay, A.M. Bowie, R. Johnstone, T. Smith, H. McGill, R. Lowrie, R. Cameron, I. Smith, W. Currie, J. McLaughlin, R. Dickson, T. Duncan (coach). Seated: J. Borland, J. McGowan, I. Fallis, J. Kennedy, I.G. Harnett (president), F.C. Thomson (captain), A. McNaughton, F. Thomson, J. Inglis.

Queen's Park v. Clyde at Hampden. A Second Division League match on 30 October 1976 – Queen's suffered a 4-0 defeat. Bernie Donnelly of Queen's is beaten to the ball by Clyde's centre half, whilst Alan Mackin of Queen's jumps in anticipation.

Queen's Park *v.* Stirling Albion at Hampden. Second Division League game which Queen's won 2-1. A well-struck shot past the Stirling Albion defenders is admired by Bernie Donnelly, Iain Campbell and Jamie Paton.

Queen's Park *v.* Clyde on New Year's Day, 1977. Gerry Colgan scores a penalty in the game against Clyde at Shawfield Stadium which resulted in a 3-3 draw. Clyde FC have since moved to their new ground at Broadwood Stadium, Cumbernauld.

Girvan Amateurs *v.* Queen's Park at Girvan, Ayrshire in a first round Scottish Cup tie against Girvan Amateurs on 8 January 1977. Left half Alan Mackin (Queen's Park) heads home the opening goal in a 3-0 victory for Queen's Park.

Queen's Park *v.* Alloa Athletic at Hampden in the third round Scottish Cup tie on 29 January 1977. In spite of appearances, Bernie Donnelly's header did not find the net in the game, which finished 0-0. Jamie Paton and Alan Mackin are also on hand as the Alloa defenders look on. Alloa won the replay 1-0.

Queen's Park *v.* Dunfermline Athletic at Hampden in a Second Division League match on 12 February 1977. Jim Nicholson scores with a classic diving header in a 3-0 win for Queen's.

Stenhousemuir *v.* Queen's Park at Ochilview Park in a Second Division League match on 26 February 1977. The Stenhousemuir goalkeeper makes a save, with Jamie Paton following up in case of any slip-up. Jim Nicholson, who scored Queen's only goal in a 2-1 defeat, watches on along with the Stenhousemuir defence.

Right: Alan Irvine, a stylish outside right with a good turn of speed. He spent four seasons with Queen's Park from 1977/78 to 1980/81, making 92 first-team appearances. He turned professional with Everton, where he had a very successful career, and is currently (2006) a member of their coaching staff

Below: Queen's Park Football Club, season 1977/78. From left to right, back row: Sam McNaughton (kit), Jim Nicholson, Ronnie Anderson, Alastair Bowie, Iain Campbell, Bobby Cameron, Alan Mackin, Bernie Donnelly, Robert McSkimming, Sandy McEwan (physiotherapist), Joe Gilroy (coach). Front row: Alan McDonald, Jamie Paton, Dougie Wilkie, Jim Rooney, Bobby Dickson, Derek Wood, Tony Glavin.

Vale of Leithen *v.* Queen's Park at Victoria Park, Innerleithen. The third round of the Scottish Cup on 28 January 1978. Alan Horn (Queen's Park) unleashes a shot for goal. Dougie Wilkie scored the only goal in Queen's 1-0 victory.

Falkirk *v.* Queen's Park at Brockville Park. Second Division League match on 25 February 1978. Alan Horn evades a sliding tackle from the Falkirk defender to get a shot on target in this game which Queen's won 3-0.

Meadowbank Thistle *v.* Queen's Park at the Meadowbank Stadium, Edinburgh in a Second Division League match on 14 October 1978. This game, which Queen's Park won 4-0, took place at the stadium which hosted the athletic events for the 1970 Commonwealth Games in Edinburgh. Ian Ballantyne of Queen's Park scores a headed goal despite the challenge of a Meadowbank Thistle defender. Derek Wood looks on.

Meadowbank Thistle were previously the works team of the Ferranti Electronic Company, playing under the name of Ferranti Thistle. In turn, Meadowbank Thistle became Livingston FC, gaining promotion to the Scottish Premier League in 2001 until the end of season 2005/06, when they were relegated.

Player of the Year award, 1978/79. The Queen's Park Supporters' Association holds an annual presentation based on votes made by the supporters. Bob Crampsey (centre), broadcaster and club historian, presented the awards to Dougie Wilkie (right) as Player of the Year and Ian Ballantyne (left) as Away Player of the Year.

Eddie Hunter. A strong-tackling defender who made a total of 263 appearances for the club from 1964/65 to 1973/74, he scored 28 goals in the process. He was head coach of the team for fifteen years, from April 1979 until December 1994, and led them to Championship success, winning the Scottish League Second Division title in season 1980/81. The next two seasons were spent in the First Division, followed by relegation to the Second Division. He has a long association with the club, stretching over twenty-five years as player and coach.

Dundee United *v.* Queen's Park at Tannadice Park, Dundee. Scottish League Cup tie on 10 October 1979. Derek Wood of Queen's Park and Frank Kopel of Dundee United take part in an aerial battle for the ball. Dundee United won 2-1 with Matt Thomson scoring Queen's goal.

Queen's Park season 1979/80. From left to right, standing: J Gillies (match secretary), S. McNaughton (assistant trainer), P. McLean, J. McGregor, J. Gillespie, D. Atkins, M. Gillespie, A. Rennie, B. Reynolds, A. McEwan (physiotherapist), N. Hopper (assistant to coach), E. Hunter (coach). Seated: R. McSkimming, A. Irvine, R. McFarlane, J. Sinclair, W.S. Burgess (president), R. Dickson, F. Melrose, G. McCoy, D. Wood.

Queen's Park v. Celtic at Hampden in the Glasgow Cup tie on 14 August 1979. Mick Gillespie drives the ball past his teammates Frank Melrose and Jim Nicholson to score Queen's Park's only goal in their 3-1 defeat. Danny McGrain, Johanes Edvaldson and Tom McAdam are the Celtic defenders.

Queen's Park at Hampden, Glasgow Cup tie on 14 August 1979. Alan Sneddon, Celtic's right-back, looks on as Frank Melrose and Alan Rennie of Queen's Park tussle with Johanes Evaldson for the ball.

seven

Initial Success/Normal Service Resumed, the 1980s

Queen's Park, season 1980/81. From left to right, back row: A. McEwan (physiotherapist), J. McGregor, S. Cook, A. Irvine, J. Nicholson, D. Atkins, M. Gillespie, R. McSkimming, A. Rennie, J. McNiven, S. McNaughton (kit). Front row: G. Crawley, G. McCoy, J. Sinclair, R. Dickson, R. McFarlane, E. Hunter (coach).
   This was the title-winning season for Queen's Park, with Derek Atkins, goalkeeper, and Jim Nicholson, forward, both ever-present in the League campaign. Gerry McCoy was the top scorer with 17 League goals.

East Stirling *v.* Queen's Park at Firs Park, Falkirk. A Second Division match on 29 March 1980 with the East Stirling players wearing their black and white hooped shirts. Mick Gillespie climbs above the East Stirling defenders to head high and wide. The home team won 3-1 on this occasion.

East Fife *v.* Queen's Park at Bayview Park, Methil. In this Second Division League match on 15 November 1980, Gerry Crawley's shot seems to be going wide according to teammate Jimmy Sinclair's reaction. The goals came from full-back Bobby Dickson and Gerry McCoy in the 2-0 win.

Queen's *v.* Cowdenbeath at Hampden. Second Division League game on 25 April 1981 with Gerry McCoy scoring the promotion-winning goal for season 1980/81. His goal in the 1-1 draw was enough to gain the point required to win the Championship. Jim Nicholson looks on.

The Queen's Park players, with Mick Gillespie and Alan Irvine to the fore, showing off the Second Division trophy to their supporters in the North Enclosure at Hampden Park.

The Queen's Park Football Club

Founded 1867

Official Programme

PRICE
10p

Programme from Queen's Park *v.* Cowdenbeath, 25 August 1981, autographed by the players of the Second Division Championship squad, season 1980/81.

Queen's Park *v.* Clydebank at Hampden. Scottish League Cup tie on 8 August 1981. The first competitive game of the 1981/82 season, with John McNiven scoring Queen's goal in the 1-1 draw.

Queen's Park *v.* Clydebank, 29 August 1981. John McGregor scores Queen's Park's first goal on return to the First Division after an absence of twenty-three years by Queen's. John McGregor was centre half and played three seasons for Queen's from 1979 to 1982 when he moved to Liverpool.

Queen's Park *v.* Falkirk at Hampden. First Division League match on 24 October 1981. Lex Grant is heading for goal against Falkirk with Benny Verrecchia 'blinded' by the power. John McGregor and John McNiven were Queen's goal scorers in the 2–2 draw.

Cartoon from the Supporters' Association notebook. 'Remember I'm in charge!'

Right: A famous personality sends a greeting to the Queen's Park Supporters' Association. Her husband, Billy Connolly, supports the other Glasgow team who sport different coloured hoops.

Below: Queen's Park *v.* Raith Rovers. First Division League game at Hampden on 12 September 1981. John McNiven out-jumps Raith's centre half to send a flashing header goalwards, but without success. The game finished scoreless.

Above: Queen's Park *v.* Motherwell at Hampden. First Division League match on 7 November 1981. Jimmy Gilmour, Queen's Park's outside left, leaves a Motherwell player trailing in his wake as he strides goalwards.

Below: Queen's Park *v.* Hibernian. Gerry Crawley in action in a pre-season friendly at Lesser Hampden against Hibernian in August 1982. Gerry Crawley toured Indonesia, Malaysia and Japan with Middlesex Wanderers, making two trips as captain.

Middlesex Wanderers Football Club was founded in 1905 to foster friendship amongst other football clubs throughout the world by sending British players abroad. Many Queen's Park players have been selected for summer tours over the years.

Above: Queen's Park *v.* Rangers at Hampden. Scottish Cup quarter-final tie on 12 March 1983. Ian Redford of Rangers clears the ball from Jim Nicholson and John McNiven of Queen's Park. Craig Paterson and Jim Bett of Rangers are also pictured.

Queen's Park played particularly well in front of a 14,000 crowd, losing by the narrow margin of 2-1. Jimmy Gilmour scored Queen's Park's goal from the penalty spot.

Below: Queen's Park *v.* Rangers at Hampden. Scottish Cup quarter-final tie on 12 March 1983. Gerry Crawley and David Graham of Queen's Park battle for possession with Robert Prytz of Rangers.

Queen's Park v. Airdrie at Hampden. First Division League match on 9 April 1983. Lex Grant takes part in a heading duel with the Airdrie defenders, Jim March and Gerry McLauchlan, whilst Ian Gordon and Tom McCartney of Airdrie look on. Queen's won the game 4-3 thanks to goals from Jim Nicholson, Jimmy Gilmour and two from Jimmy Quinn.

Queen's Park v. Corinthian Casuals. Centenary match, Hampden Park, 30 July 1983, with the result 0-0. Queen's Park played Corinthians in recognition of their 100 years' existence. The Corinthians were all soccer playing ex-public school pupils. Formed in England in 1882, their aim was to uphold the values of the amateur game. It was appropriate that they should take on Queen's Park in annual challenge matches which took place from 1 January 1886 until 1936, with the New Year's Day game played at Hampden Park and the return games at various venues in London, including Crystal Palace and Queen's Club. Seventy games were played over the fifty-year period, then in 1939 the Corinthians amalgamated with the Casuals to form Corinthian Casuals FC.

Above: Queen's Park 1983/84 season. From left to right, back row: S. McNaughton (assistant), A. McEwan (physiotherapist), S. Cook, A. Rennie, J. Quinn, S. Ross, A. Grant, K. Brannigan, G. Wilson, J. McNiven, I. Campbell (assistant coach), E. Hunter (coach). Front row: W. Cairns, G. Fraser, J. Nicholson, T. Barr (president), J. Ward, J. Gilmour, F. Loughran.

Below: Stirling Albion *v.* Queen's Park at Annfield, Stirling. Second Division League match on 17 September 1983. Joe Woods heads clear with a Stirling attacker paying close attention whilst David Hunter and David Graham of Queen's Park keep a close watch on John Colquhoun (no.7) of Stirling. Queen's lost 1-0.

Albion Rovers *v.* Queen's Park at Cliftonhill, Coatbridge. In this Second Division League match on 7 April 1984, which resulted in a 0-0 draw, Desi Walker shoots for goal.

Queen's Park, 1984/85 season. Left to right, back row: J. Nicholson, W. Cairns, S. Ross, P.G. McLaughlin, M.A. Smith. Middle row: A. McEwan (physiotherapist), D.G. McKay, R. Caven, K. Brannigan, J.F. Ward, G.C. Crooks, E. Hunter (coach). Front row: S. McNaughton (kit), I. McCall, G. Fraser, T. Barr (president), D.J. Walker, J. Boyle, I. Campbell (assistant coach).

Queen's Park *v.* East Stirling at Hampden. Second Division match on 18 August 1984. Ross Caven, Queen's centre forward, celebrating one of his two goals in the 4-1 defeat of East Stirling. Ian McCall also somewhat pleased with the outcome.

Queen's Park *v.* Queen of the South at Hampden. Second Division match on 2 March 1985. Mark Smith hurdles a Queen of the South defender whilst his teammate Gary Fraser follows up.

Queen's Park *v.* Dunfermline at Hampden. Second Division League match on 24 August 1985. Ian McCall (Queen's Park) flicking the ball over Ian Westwater, Dunfermline's goalkeeper, to score one of Queen's Park's goals in a 3-1 win.

Celtic *v.* Queen's Park at Celtic Park in the Scottish Cup fourth round on 15 February 1986. Stevie Ross, Queen's Park's goalkeeper, and teammate Jimmy Boyle in action against Mo Johnston (Celtic). Queen's opened the scoring with a penalty scored by Jimmy Boyle and, although Queen's played very well, they were eventually defeated 2-1.

Right: Ross Caven in typical climbing mode in the game against Ayr United at Hampden on 21 November 1987.

Below: A squad of Queen's Park ball boys for the 1986/87 season. Queen's Park ball boys are on duty at Hampden Park for every home game. In addition, they are on duty for all other important games such as the Scottish Cup final, Scotland international games and in 2002 for the Champions League final between Real Madrid and Bayer Leverkusen.

The familiar facade of the South Stand at Hampden Park. The stand was finally demolished in the late 1990s to make way for the present BT South Stand.

eight

Third Division times, the 1990s

Queen's Park 1991/92 season. From left to right, back row: S. Jack, S. McEntegart, R. Caven, M. Mackay, S. McCormick, M. Flannigan, J. O'Brien. Middle Row: S. McNaughton (kit), J. Rodden, D. Moonie, B. Findlay (physiotherapist), J. Chalmers, D. Jackson, M.A. Hay (assistant coach). Seated: G. Orr, G. Elder, E. Hunter (coach), M.B. Smith (president), J. O'Neill, C. Stevenson.

Above: Queen's Park Football Club committee, 1991/92. From left to right, back row: P.G. Buchanan, R.L. Cromar, W.S. Burgess, M.D. Mackay, I.G. Harnett, W. Omand. Front row: T. Barr, W.L. Ross, (treasurer), M.B. Smith (president), A. Reilly, J.C. Rutherford (secretary).

The Queen's Park committee comprises mainly ex-players. The committee pictured is a fine representation of the group of men who have served the club following the founders' aim to promote football.

Queen's Park *v.* Stirling Albion. Mick Monaghan, Queen's Park's goalkeeper, makes a fine diving save against Stirling Albion at Annfield.

Above: John O'Neill scoring his eighteenth goal of the 1993/94 season against Meadowbank Thistle on 16 April 1994.

Opposite below: Queen's Park *v.* Clyde. A crowded goalmouth with Ross Caven climbing above everyone to reach the ball in this Scottish Cup tie at Hampden Park on 4 December 1992.

Steve McCormick out-jumping Arbroath's keeper to score in the 2-1 victory at Hampden on 5 February 1994.

Brian McPhee rounds Arbroath's keeper on the stroke of half-time only to blast the ball against the crossbar. Arbroath went on to win 4-0 on 19 November 1994.

David Graham's well-taken penalty kick was competently saved by Alloa's goalkeeper, Robert Balfour, to deny Queen's the win. The non-scoring draw took place on 7 October 1995.

Graeme Elder, seen here on the right, rushes in hoping to score against Inverness Caledonian Thistle, but is denied by a last-ditch clearance by a Caley defender. The game took place on 23 November 1996 and, in spite of a second-half two-goal comeback, Queen's went down 3-2.

Hampden Park was under reconstruction during the winter of 1997. The South Stand and rooftop press box have been demolished to leave a huge gap in the stadium. The players warm up in very open conditions for the Scottish Cup tie against Gala Fairydean on 4 January 1997.

Later in 1997, the gap is being filled in with the frame of the new South Stand.

John McCormack was appointed as head coach of Queen's Park on 15 June 1998. This was the first time in Queen's Park history that a full-time coach had been appointed. It was to prove an inspired appointment.

Malky Mackay, jnr. was a commanding centre half who followed in his father's footsteps to play for Queen's Park. He moved to Celtic, then Norwich City, where he gained his first of five Scotland caps when he was selected to play against Denmark. He gained a further four international caps for Scotland against Estonia, Trinidad & Tobago, Spain and Slovenia respectively.

Queen's Park, season 1999/00. From left to right, back row: F. Carroll, R. Sinclair, R. Caven, B. Rossiter, J. Whelan, S. Orr, M. Gallagher, R. Scobie, P. Borland, B. McColl, K. Finlayson. Centre row: R. Cant (coach), D. McKenzie (physiotherapist), J. Brown, M. Travers, G. Connell, P. Ferguson, P. Martin, (captain), C. McKee, N. MacFarlane, D. Carmichael, P. Walker, B. Sweeney (coach). Front row: W. Neil (kit), A. Hutchison (club doctor), D. Graham, D. Connaghan, A. Smith, J. McCormack (head coach), J. Nicholson (president), N. Inglis, D. Ferry, K. McGoldrick, R. Findlay (physiotherapist), D. Hunter (coach).

Opposite above: Queen's Park's minibus. Robin Barr, chairman of Irn-Bru, Scotland's other national drink, presents a minibus to be used by Queen's Park's youth teams. Danny Ferry and Willie Martin hitch a lift. Irn-Bru have faithfully supported Queen's Park for many years and so Queen's Park's away strip colours of blue and orange are those of Irn-Bru.

Opposite below: The reconstruction of Hampden Park was completed in May 1999. A Gala night took place on the evening of 21 May 1999, attracting a crowd of 20,000 to mark the reopening of the stadium. This included a game between a Queen's Park Former Players XI and an International Celebrity XI. The Celebrities All Stars XI, which included Rod Stewart and Kenny Dalglish, won 2-0, with goals scored by Kenny Dalglish and Frank McDougall.

Rod Stewart receives some close attention from Eddie Hunter and Jim Hastie of Queen's Park, whilst Tommy Burns looks on with interest.

A group shot of the Queen's Park players celebrating their triumph at Cowdenbeath.

Unfurling the Third Division Championship 1999/00 flag at Hampden Park. Jim Nicholson, club president, is pictured with Peter Donald, Scottish League secretary, Lord McFarlane of Bearsden KT, hon. patron, and Alistair MacKay, club secretary.

nine

2000 and Beyond

Queen's Park *v.* Berwick Rangers. Kevin Finlayson (Queen's Park) trying to evade a strong tackle from a Berwick Rangers defender. This was Queen's first home game at Hampden Park on 5 August 2000, following their promotion to the Scottish Football League Second Division. The team made a winning start by 1-0, with Stephen Marshall scoring the goal.

Above: Queen's Park *v.* Forfar Athletic. Frankie Carroll (Queen's Park) gains possession from a Forfar Athletic player in the game at Hampden Park on 21 October 2000 which finished goalless. At this stage of the season, after playing eleven games, Queen's Park were lying in third place in the League behind Clydebank and Partick Thistle.

Left: Ross Caven made his first-team debut against Hamilton Academical on 14 August 1982 at the age of eighteen. He later became a first-team regular in 1984/85 and is pictured celebrating his first ever League goal against East Stirlingshire on 14 August 1984 in Queen's Park's 4-1 victory. He made his last appearance on 19 March 2002. By that time, he had made the club record of 594 appearances, scoring a total of 103 goals. It is unlikely that his record will ever be surpassed at the club.

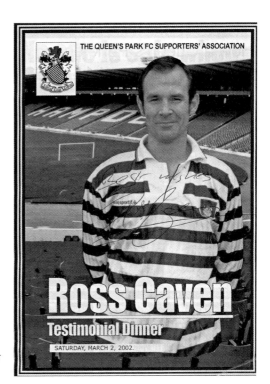

Programme cover for the Queen's Park Supporters' Association testimonial dinner held on behalf of Ross Caven. On 2 March 2002, the supporters paid tribute by hosting a dinner to mark Ross Caven's playing career which spanned almost twenty years.

Queen's Park *v*. Everton. A pre-season friendly on 23 July 2002 at Hampden Park heralded the first-team debut of a sixteen-year-old Wayne Rooney who had only made four reserve-team games for Everton. He is pictured being held off by Damiano Agostini (Queen's Park). Wayne Rooney scored an impressive three of Everton's goals in his club's 6-0 victory. He has progressed to being an important member of England's international team.

Civic Dinner

To celebrate the

Centenary of Hampden Park

on

Thursday 15 January 2004

The City Chambers
Glasgow

Above: Front cover of the menu for the civic dinner held on 15 January 2004 to celebrate the centenary of Hampden Park.

Left: The club held its own dinner at Hampden Park to celebrate the stadium's 100th birthday. Denis Law is one of the guests displaying a Queen's Park jersey. Such a pity that he could not be coaxed to make a comeback for The Spiders.

Queen's Park programmes have been produced to a high standard. The club programme won the Division Three Programme of the Year, season 2002/03.

Billy Stark, head coach of Queen's Park. Billy Stark was appointed head coach on 30 August 2004. A skilful midfielder, he played for St. Mirren, Aberdeen, Celtic and Kilmarnock. During his four years at Aberdeen, he gained two Scottish League Championship medals, two Scottish Cup medals, one Scottish League Cup medal, appeared in the semi-final of the European Cup-Winners' Cup and the quarter-final of the European Cup. Whilst playing in the Scottish Premier League, he scored more than 100 goals. He was assistant coach at Hamilton Academical, Kilmarnock and Celtic before moving on to be the manager at Greenock Morton and then at St Johnstone FC.

Paul Harvey (Queen's Park) striding up the wing against Albion Rovers at Hampden on his way to bamboozle one of the Albion Rovers defenders. A 1-1 draw was the outcome with Ross Clark scoring Queen's goal. Paul Harvey brought a wealth of experience to a young squad of players.

Spiders against racism. On 16 October 2004 the players from the Active Life Club helped Queen's Park and the Scottish League to mark the official launch of the Show Racism the Red Card campaign.

Queen's Park encouraged women's football, with the Queen's Park Ladies becoming runners-up to Glasgow City in the 2004 Scottish Cup. Included in the line-up are: Allison Gormley, Tina Ferguson, Dani Stewart, Lyn Walton, Amy McDonald, Siobhan Paterson, Lorna Gray, Lesley Condie, Amanda Craig, Caroline Jamieson, Alanah Murphy, Sabrina Duncan.

Caroline Jamieson of Queen's Park Ladies in action.

Queen's Park in the community. From November 2005, Billy Stark became a full-time employee of the club. His duties include his participation in a new community initiative to strengthen links with youngsters from all ethnic groups and, as can be seen here, his continued involvement in football development.

Queen's Park, season 2005/06. From left to right, back row: P. Paton, L. McCann, S. Canning, S. Kettlewell, A. Cowie, D. Crawford, M. Cairns, M. Ferry, S. Molloy, D. Weatherston, R. Bowers. Middle row: W. Ogilvie (kit manager), R. Cant (goalkeeping coach), A. Trouten, S. Reilly, A. McGinty, M. Dunlop, J. Weir, A. Quinn, D. Agostini, J. Whelan, K. Proctor, B. Felvus, A.S. Hutchison (doctor), R. Findlay (physiotherapist). Front row: D. McCallum (assistant coach), T. Murray, P. Harvey, W. Stark (coach), G. Templeman (president), R. Sinclair (club captain), R. Clark, R. Dickson (assistant coach).

Stuart Kettlewell, Richard Sinclair and Damiano Agostini of Queen's Park deal with the threat of Stevie Crawford of Aberdeen in the CIS second-round tie at Firhill Stadium on 22 August 2006. The tie was held at Partick Thistle's ground as the Rolling Stones concert was to take place at Hampden Park. It was an inspired game by the young amateurs of Queen's Park who defeated their Premier League opponents. The score after extra time remained 0-0, however, a series of confidently taken penalties, including one by goalkeeper Mark Cairns, resulted in a 5-3 win for Queen's and a victory which will be savoured for many a day by the players and supporters of Queen's Park. 'C'mon the Spiders!'

Other titles published by STADIA

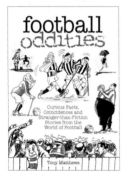

Wizards and Bravehearts A History of the Scottish National Side
DAVID POTTER

The history of Scotland's national football team from 1872 is full of highs and lows, thrills and heartbreaks, passion and pride. Read the stories of Scotland – including the 1920s when they were undubitably the best in the world, the sad underperformances of the 1950s and '60s and the disasters of Argentina in 1978. This is a must for every Scottish football fan.

0 7524 4183 8

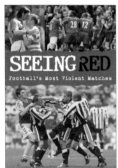

Football Oddities
TONY MATTHEWS

In one of the most individual and irreverent collections of footballing facts ever produced, Tony Matthews has unearthed tales of the unexpected that will delight footy fans everywhere. Did you hear the one about the Argentine full-back who scored a hat-trick of own goals in less than an hour? Remember the England goalkeeper who was sent off after just twenty-seven seconds of a Premiership game in 1995? Read about them – and many, many others – here.

0 7524 3401 2

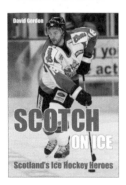

Seeing Red Football's Most Violent Matches
PHIL THOMPSON

It is a fact that football and fighting are all too frequent bedfellows. Competitive spirit leading to anger – and then to violence – is not a new facet to the game. In fact, unpalatable though it may seem, it is part of football's history. This book explores some of the most violent games of all time. Violent challenges, tactics of foul play and ill-conditioned manners, they are all here. Upfront and honest, this is a telling insight into the ugly side of the beautiful game

0 7524 3778 X

Scotch on Ice Scotland's Ice Hockey Heroes
DAVID GORDON

Throughout the sport's history, many of the finest ice hockey players produced by these islands have hailed from Scotland. The players featured in this book, all GB internationals, with several also being members of the British Hall of Fame, are some of the finest ever seen on Scottish ice. Recalling the ups and downs of their time in the game, author David Gordon has delved beyond the 'hockey player' tag to reveal something of the men themselves.

0 7524 3801 8

If you are interested in purchasing other books published by Stadia, or in case you have difficulty finding any Stadia books in your local bookshop, you can also place orders directly through the Tempus Publishing website
www.tempus-publishing.com